The **Essential** Buyer's Guide
Velocette
350 & 500
1946-1970

AF190529

Your marque expert:
Peter Henshaw

VELOCE PUBLISHING
THE PUBLISHER OF FINE AUTOMOTIVE BOOKS

www.Veloce.co.uk

For post publication news, updates and amendments relating to this book please scan the QR code or visit www.veloce.co.uk/books/V4941

First published in November 2016 by Veloce Publishing Limited, Veloce House, Parkway Farm Business Park, Middle Farm Way, Poundbury, Dorchester, Dorset, DT1 3AR, England.
Fax 01305 250479/e-mail info@veloce.co.uk/web www.veloce.co.uk or www.velocebooks.com.

ISBN: 978-1-845849-41-2 UPC: 6-36847-04941-6

Introduction

– the purpose of this book

If you want to buy a Velocette single, then you are about to join one of the smallest, yet most committed owner groups of all. When they were new, Velocettes inspired great loyalty amongst a small band of riders who loved their idiosyncratic ways, and exactly the same is true today.

Modern day advocates will tell you that Velo singles combine the superb build quality of a Sunbeam, the fine handling of a Norton, and the mechanical strength of a Rudge; and there is some truth in that. Velocettes were quite unlike the mass produced singles from BSA or Matchless, being carefully built in a relatively small factory from quality components.

Velocettes are British bike thoroughbreds, but they're not all the same.

Mechanically quiet, they had (and still do have) the high speed stamina that some British classics lack. They are also relatively light, and handle very well, something reflected in a whole string of racing successes, right into the 1960s when they were apparently obsolete: Velocettes won the first Production TT in 1967, several long distance circuit races and, in 1961, set a 24-hour speed record that, for 500cc bikes, still stands.

On the other hand, those less enamoured of the Velocette legend would counter that they leak oil like the proverbial sieve, that they are overpriced, overrated and need more than a certain knack to kickstart. Clutch adjustment is seen as a black art, while the electrics belong to a different (and extremely dim) era. To own a Velocette, these people say, you need to be a professional engineer with a well-equipped workshop.

3

As ever, the truth lies somewhere between these extremes. All those good points are absolutely true: Velocettes are strong and are great fun on twisty roads, but they also need the sympathetic ownership that any classic bike demands, with particular attention paid to starting technique, clutch adjustment and the electrics.

The Velocette company personified British four-stroke singles in a very individual way.

If you haven't been put off yet, then this book is a straightforward, practical guide to buying a Velocette single. It won't list all the correct colours for each year, or analyse the bikes' design philosophy, company background or racing record (there are excellent books and websites listed at the end of this book that do all that) but hopefully it will help you avoid buying a dud.

Although the typical Velocette single is often seen as a sporting, and potentially cantankerous, Thruxton or Venom, the most popular bike – the factory made 25,000 of them – was the mildly tuned, long-stroke MAC 350 from which they were derived. It's the Velocette that's easiest to live with, and a good starting point for anyone who wants to sample the Velo experience. But the MAC is not fast, the 500cc MSS, either pre-1948 long-stroke guise or from 1954-on offers more mid-range power. Faster still, at least when revved, are the more highly tuned Viper 350 and Venom 500, plus their Clubman variants. Some see the final Venom Thruxton as the ultimate Velocette, though it's also the most demanding to own, as well as the most expensive. Velocette built just 1108 Thruxtons, but if that's not rare enough, the brash Indian Velo is a rare beast indeed, as is the unsuccessful factory Scrambler.

Whichever Velocette you decide on, you will be buying one of the British industry's most recognisable and idiosyncratic motorcycles, something that will reward sympathetic ownership. You certainly won't forget it!

This book would not have been possible without the help of several people: Velocette owners Pat Clancy and Alan Deacon allowed me to photograph their bikes and pick their brains about the ins and outs of Velocette ownership. Justin Harvey-James and the staff of the Vintage Motorcycle Club were very helpful in providing the Club's library for research. Thanks also go to Roger Fogg.

Contents

1 Is it the right bike for you?
– marriage guidance

Like most classic bikes, Velocettes are small and light compared to big modern machines. They have a relatively low seat, especially in the case of the pre-1953 rigid frame models; which is good news for shorter riders.

Running costs
Not huge. Like many older four-stroke singles, Velos are surprisingly economical (50-70mpg or more). All of them (the MAC in particular) are relatively easy on consumable items such as tyres, brake linings, chains and sprockets.

Maintenance
Intensive and ongoing, rather than sticking to rigid service intervals. Living with a Velocette demands looking out for it, being on the alert to anything that needs attention.

Kick starting
Velocettes have a reputation for being difficult starters, even by the standards of big four-stroke singles, the combination of a short, low-geared kickstart and occasional clutch slip compound the challenge. A MAC in good condition is easy to start; however, the higher compression Thruxton and Venom can be awkward.

Usability
Thruxton apart (with its radical clip-ons and rear sets), the Velos are quite useable bikes, tractable at low speed, and have a comfortable riding position; and they can manage sustained higher speeds, if you can stand some vibration.

Parts availability
Very good, parts supply has improved as Velocettes have become more collectable, and more money has been put into keeping them on the road. Only big items such as crankcases aren't available new, and these may be offered in the future.

Parts costs
Reasonable, despite their rarified and upmarket image, Velos are no more expensive to buy parts for than equivalent British classics.

Insurance group
Go for a classic bike limited mileage policy, such as that offered by Carole Nash or Footman James in the UK, and you shouldn't pay much for insurance.

Investment potential
Velocettes are a safe investment, because they are very unlikely ever to go down in value, and are still rising, though not dramatically. The Thruxton will always command the highest price.

Foibles
The Velocette clutch certainly counts as a foible; the design is unique to Velocette, sensitive to correct adjustment, and easy to maladjust.

Plus points
There are many. Velocettes are good to ride and make a lovely noise. There's the Velocette Owners Club, which is active, supportive to new owners, whose members have amassed many years of living with the big singles.

Minus points
Velocettes, with the exception of the MAC, are expensive, and a bread and butter single from BSA (Gold Star excepted), Matchless or AJS will be cheaper.

Alternatives
In terms of 'cooking' four-stroke singles, there are plenty of alternatives, all of which, arguably, have less charisma than a Velocette: AJS/Matchless, BSA, Ariel, OHV Nortons, the list goes on. High-performance alternatives are the BSA Gold Star and overhead cam Norton singles, but Norton dropped its OHC bikes in 1957, and BSA the Gold Star in '63 – henceforth, Velocette was the only high-performance single still available.

These bikes are relatively small and light, but they won't suit everyone.

2 Cost considerations
– affordable, or a money pit?

There is a good spares supply for Velocettes – as well as the specialists, the Velocette Owners Club has its own spares scheme, and prices for routine items are good value, though specialist conversions parts like a 12-volt alternator are more expensive. The prices here are from an independent specialist, for a mix of models. If you are about to buy your first Velocette, it's well worth joining the club, which will help any new owners.

Complete restoration (basket case to concours) – around ●x8000
Alternator (Alton 12v conversion) – ●x330
Ammeter – ●x26
Brake shoes (front, each) – ●x16
Battery – ●x12.50
Carburettor (Amal Monobloc) – ●x145
Chain – ●x43
Clutch plates (ea) – ●x16
Downpipe – ●x69
Dynamo brushes – ●x8.50
Exhaust downpipe – ●x69
Flywheel assembly – ●x820
Fork oil seals (ea) – ●x4
Fork stanchions (ea) – ●x65
Gasket set – ●x17

Headlight glass/reflector – ●x30
Light switch – ●x45
Magneto (BTH, electronic) – ●x500
Mudguard (rear) – ●x149
Mudguard stay (front) – ●x14
Piston – ●x129
Primary chain – ●x29
Pushrod – ●x20
Rear shocks (pr, Woodhead-Monroe) – ●x125
Dual seat – ●x160
Silencer – ●x138
Valves (ea) – ●x22
Wheel bearing – ●x9.50
Wheel rim (chrome) – ●x91
Wiring loom – ●x36

Consumable parts aren't expensive.

Most spares are available, through specialists or the Velocette Owners' Club.

3 Living with a Velocette

– will you get along together?

Whether or not you will get along with a Velocette depends on which one you end up buying. There's a world of difference between the soft and easy-going MAC – which is a 350cc tourer in the traditional mould – and the high compression, street racing Thruxton, as the latter is much harder to live with. Whichever Velocette you choose, if it's your first classic, there are some general points to bear in mind.

Modern bikes don't need a lot of attention between scheduled services – maybe just an engine oil check and chain adjustment – but classic bikes (Velocettes, in particular) aren't like that. Maintenance is more of an ongoing process, always keeping an eye open for nuts and bolts coming loose, blown bulbs or tappet adjustment. That's not to say that these things happen all the time, but it's good practice to be on the lookout. It might sound like a chore, but for some people it's one of the attractions of owning a classic. You develop a relationship with it; one that you don't get with a modern bike that always starts on the button and never goes wrong.

With a Velocette, you have to adapt yourself to the bike, both in the way you ride it and the way you look after it. Take the brakes and electrics: Velocette stuck with six-volt electrics to the end, and the Miller system didn't have a great reputation when new, the dynamo giving out a modest 36 watts (compared to 180 watts from a typical modern bike). There are plenty of ways to upgrade the system – to 12 volts, with an electronic magneto and regulator – and unless that's been done, don't plan on any long overnight rides. The brakes did improve over the years, and the final twin leading-shoe front drum is pretty good, but the early 7in half-width hub drum is weak for modern traffic. However, again, upgrades are relatively easy to do – many earlier bikes have the later full-width hub or TLS brake.

Kickstarting is something else you will have to come to terms with, unless you can afford the Alton electric start conversion. Velocettes have a fearsome reputation for difficult starting, and there is some basis for that. The kickstart mechanism is low-geared, so kicking over the engine won't have it spinning very fast. The short kickstart lever compounds this by reducing leverage, and if the clutch is slipping (not uncommon) then that makes life even more difficult. But as ever with kickstarting, success has more to do with technique than sheer strength. The low compression MAC and MSS are actually quite easy to start, given the correct technique and with everything in good condition. The higher compression bikes are certainly challenging, with the Venom/Viper, their Clubman variants and the Thruxton, in increasing order of difficulty. Even here, there can be more differences between individual bikes than between models.

It's also worth remembering that because different models share the same basic format, it's easy to upgrade (say, an MSS into a Venom) so check that the mild tourer you've set your heart on hasn't been fitted with a high compression piston.

Oil leaks are almost a fact of life, especially from the primary drive case and pushrod tube, though oil tightness was much improved by the better breathing system fitted from 1967. Again, caring owners may have retro-fitted this to an earlier bike. The Velo clutch is perhaps more of a challenge, because even when it's set up perfectly you still need to use it sympathetically, slipping into neutral before stopping. When set up right, it is a good clutch, light and positive, but adjustment needs patience and the ability to follow instructions.

Having read all of this, you may decide that a Velocette sounds like too much trouble. But read on, because there are lots of good things about them that make the mechanical foibles worth enduring. *Classic Motorcycle* author Steve Wilson once described Velo singles as, "... strong, fast, long-legged thoroughbreds," and that's exactly what they are.

A Velocette in good shape can be a joy to ride, as they handle very well, and the big single has lots of mid-range power, (less so on the highly-tuned Thruxton) but it's also very tractable. Although the early front brakes are weak, the later full-width hubs (and better still, the final twin leading-shoe set-up) are pretty good.

As mentioned, Velocettes are mechanically strong; able to sustain high speeds without falling apart. This is partly down to the design: a narrow, rigid crankcase with a fully pressed up crankshaft, and short, stiff pushrods. That also makes them long-lived, and mileages of 100,000 have been achieved before serious bottom end work was needed.

And because the gearing is high, the bikes feel relaxed when ridden hard, with just that solid, thumping exhaust note from the distinctive fishtail silencer, memorably described by journalist Peter Watson as, "Mellow as a 12-year-old Scotch and as solid as rump steak." Velocettes aren't frenetic, but all the 500s can maintain a decent turn of speed whilst loping across the countryside.

In short, although these bikes do need careful and considerate ownership – and some aspects, such as starting and clutch adjustment, will involve a learning curve for any new owner – the rewards they give come in spades.

4 Relative values
– which model for you?

Range availability

MAC & early MSS
1934-39, 1946-60 MAC
1935-39, 1946-48 MSS

Later MSS, Viper & Venom
1954-70 MSS
1956-68 Viper
1956-68 Venom
1959-68 Viper Sports
1959-68 Venom Sports
1960-66 Viper Clubman

1960-66 Venom Clubman
1963-68 Viper Special
1963-68 Venom Special
1967-68 Viper Clubman MkII
1967-70 Venom Clubman MkII

Venom Thruxton
1965-70 Venom Thruxton

Specials
1969-71 Indian Velo 500

All values are relative to the MAC/early MSS

MAC & early MSS
The 350cc MAC is thought to be the easiest Velocette single to get on with, and the best choice for anyone looking to buy their first one. It's also the most numerous, with over 22,000 built over a long production run, though just as many Venoms seem to be on the market now.

A MAC is a good Velocette to start with.

Its origins lie with the 1933 MOV, a 250cc single that pioneered the familiar layout of a high camshaft engine with short pushrods and narrow crankcases, using almost square bore/stroke dimensions of 68 x 68.25mm.

The MOV was fast for its day, topping 60mph, and had good handling. Although Velocette designed it as simpler and cheaper than its exotic overhead cam K-series machines; few MOVs have survived.

Our story really starts with the MAC, launched in 1934 and sharing many parts with the little 250. A very long stroke of 96mm increased capacity to 349cc, but with the same rigid frame, girder forks and four-speed gearbox as the MOV, it weighed only 10lb more. Enclosed valve gear, automatic ignition advance, and an optional foot gear change made it more advanced than some contemporaries. And the long-stroke single proved to be surprisingly fast, with a top speed of 75mph, not much slower than the K-series. It sold well, and over 17,000 rigid frame MACs would be built up to 1953.

It was joined, in 1935, by the 499cc MSS, bored out to 81mm and housed in a new cradle frame. Top speed was only slightly higher than the MAC, but the 500 had more pulling power and was popular as a sidecar machine. This is not to be confused with the postwar (1954-on) alloy-engined MSS, which has a square 86x86mm bore/stroke.

A wartime version of the MAC, the MAF, was built during World War II, but these are now very rare. Both MAC and MSS went back into production in 1946, acquiring Dowty air forks two years later, when the MSS was dropped.

That left the MAC as the sole Velocette single, as the company concentrated its attention on the little LE flat-twin, which never fulfilled sales expectations, though the MAC continued to sell steadily. It was updated over the years, with an alloy cylinder head in 1950, conventional telescopic forks in '51 and (the big change) a swingarm frame in '53.

Basic 350 doesn't have the glamour of a Thruxton, but is charming to ride.

The MAC is almost universally acclaimed as one of the sweetest natured British singles of all – pleasant and unhurried to ride, and smoother than the bigger, more highly tuned 500s of any make. Although not very powerful (15bhp for the alloy-engined version), the long stroke gave it reasonable mid-range torque, and the MAC will pull from 20mph in top gear and happily keep up 50-55mph uphill and down, while a short wheelbase and low centre of gravity deliver good handling. The 7-inch half-width front brake was weak, though some bikes have been upgraded with later full-width hubs.

The MAC was designed to be an easy-to-live-with bike, and that certainly holds true today, at least compared to the bigger and hotter Velocettes. The 1953-on swingarm bikes are heavier, and have a higher seat than the rigid machines, but are still relatively light (355lb), easy to ride, and can top 70mph.

The swingarm MAC sold steadily through the 1950s, with about 6000 produced, and many of these have survived. Cheaper than the 500s, it makes a good first choice.

Strengths/weaknesses: The same drawbacks as all Velocettes – oil leaks, weak electrics, plus the poor front brake. It's the slowest Velo, but also the easiest to live with and most relaxing to ride. A good introduction to Velocette ownership. MAC: 100%

1946 MSS: essentially a pre-war bike with girder forks, iron head and rigid rear end.

Later MSS, Viper & Venom

If the MAC had its roots in the 1930s, then the 500cc MSS and Venom, and 350cc Viper are more typical of their heyday in the 1950s. Launched in 1954, when Velocette realised that it could not survive for long on disappointing LE sales, the new MSS was quite different to the old prewar machine. Although it shared the familiar Velo engine layout, the bore/stroke was now square (86x86mm), with alloy cylinder barrel and head, plus strengthened bottom end and gearbox. The cycle parts were similar to the swingarm MAC, apart from a bigger, 7-inch, rear brake.

The MSS was tuned for touring and hauling sidecars around, with a low 6.8:1 compression and mild valve timing. Though with the relatively short stroke and stronger bottom end it did have potential for more power – it claimed 23bhp at 5000rpm – and could reach about 80mph. Popular too, with over 9000 built, and it was offered right up to 1970, though by then sales had slowed to a trickle.

More power did arrive in 1956 with the hotter 349cc Viper and 499cc Venom; sports versions of the MSS roadster. With higher compression, a bigger carburettor, hotter cams and more radical valve timing, they offered a lot more horsepower: 27bhp for the Viper, 36bhp for the Venom. Incidentally, the Viper 350 is not to be confused with the old long-stroke MAC, being more of a downsized MSS with 72x86mm bore/stroke.

1959 MSS: now with swingarm rear end and alloy head.

Either way, the new Velocette sports roadsters are considerably faster than either MAC or MSS, with contemporary road tests quoting speeds of 92mph for the Viper, 102mph for the Venom. Fortunately, better brakes came as part of the package, with full-width hubs front and rear. While chrome mudguards and fuel tank panels with round badges set it all off, a headlight nacelle incorporated the speedo and ammeter.

Both bikes are different in character to the MAC/MSS, needing more revs to make the most of the extra power, and in fact some say the Venom is no faster than an MSS up to 4000rpm. But it takes off higher up the range, and will rev to 6000rpm, while the Viper can manage 7000 in short bursts. So, with the better brakes and already fine handling, these bikes are definitive British sports singles. Of the two, the Viper is rarer, as fewer were sold to start with (3589 against 5721 Venoms) and some were

MSS is the most relaxed of the 500cc Velos – but still good for touring.

upgraded to Venom spec by keen owners, something that was relatively easy to do. Production ended in 1968, while the Venom carried on to 1970.

So fast were the Viper and Venom that Velocette offered a race kit, which from 1960 became the Clubman package, with higher still compression, rear-set footrests, TT carburettor, BTH manual magneto, close-ratio gearbox and megaphone silencer. The handlebars were lower (though still one-piece, not clip-ons) and there was two-way damping for the forks. It's worth noting that many of these parts were fitted as individual options by the factory and that owners will have upgraded bikes in the meantime, so exact specifications are fairly fluid – the MAC and MSS for example, could be had with the Viper/Venom full-width hubs.

The Clubmen are exciting bikes to ride, even more so than the standard Viper/Venom, though they are trickier to start than an MSS, have a less certain idle and are less tractable in town. The final Clubman MkIIs from 1967 had Thruxton forks and twin-leading shoe front brake.

The MSS/Viper/Venom variant worth seeking is the option of glassfibre panelling covering the engine bottom end, gearbox, primary drive and dynamo. It looks odd now, but was a reflection of the brief fashion for panelled motorcycles at the time. The panels also saved Velocette money, as the hidden cases didn't need to be polished. Few buyers opted for panelling and many later owners threw them away, making an original glassfibre-clad Velocette very rare now. In 1963, the Viper and Venom Specials had pale blue panelling as standard, with tinwork to match, and no chrome, all to save £20-£30 on the price. These are highly collectable.

Glassfibre enclosure was a period piece, but very few have survived. (www.classicmotorbikes.net)

All hail the café racer cult – the Thruxton became a legendary part of it.

Also worth looking out for are the optional Avonaire fairing on the Viper or Venom Veeline. The originals came with touring or sports screens, and full fairing or cut down Dolphin version. New replica fairings are now available.

Strengths/weaknesses: Extra mid-range performance of MSS and top end performance of Viper/Venom, though with vibration at high revs. Usual Velocette drawbacks of poor electrics, oil leaks, the clutch. Venom/Viper more challenging to start. Of the three, MSS is the easiest to live with.

MSS: 127%
Viper: 126%
Venom: 180%

Venom Thruxton

For many, the Venom Thruxton is the ultimate Velocette. It's certainly the fastest, most powerful, and comes with the biggest slice of café racer cool, though it's difficult to ride in town and can be tricky to start. It's also the rarest Velo single, with just 1108 built between 1965 and 1970, and by far the most expensive. Other bikes may have been fitted with Thruxton parts, so if you suspect a fake, check the engine number – prefix VMT signifies a genuine factory Thruxton.

Gaining its name from a win at the 1964 Thruxton 500, a 500-mile race at the twisty Hampshire circuit, the bike was launched in June 1965, and originally described by the factory as, "… unsuitable for road use." The specification certainly hinted at the race track, though most Thruxtons (like the Clubman series) were used on the road.

The Thruxton was certainly highly tuned. A revised cylinder head brought a bigger, 2-inch inlet valve and better gas flow. There were faster-lift cam followers, a 9:1 compression (10:1 optional), an Amal GP carburettor, and the crankcases were heat treated for extra strength – the result was 41bhp at 6200rpm.

To suit, the famous clutch had 20 springs in place of the usual 16, and two-way damped forks (now with gaiters) were standard along with a new twin leading-shoe front brake – this fitted the standard drum, so it was easy to upgrade a Viper or Venom with the same brake. The Thruxton certainly looked the part, finished in silver with a long humped seat, chrome headlight (no nacelle), swept back exhaust, low Monza style bars (not clip-ons). It also featured matching speedo and rev counter, alloy rims and a large cut-out at the right-

Final Thruxtons had coil ignition, but stuck to six volts and a dynamo.

hand rear of the 4.25-gallon tank, to accommodate that GP carb. Demand from traditionalists added the familiar black/gold colour scheme from 1967.

Today, the carburettor is one of the challenges of owning a Thruxton, as it has no idle setting, though it can be converted to the more convenient Amal Concentric. The Thruxton is certainly fast (with a top speed of around 110mph) at the expense of some vibration, and the stronger clutch is said to be less likely to slip, but more likely to drag. The bike is also by far the most collectable and expensive Velocette, commanding a large premium over a standard Venom.

Strengths/weaknesses: Glamour of the ultimate supersports Velocette single, with all the period extras – also benefits from improved lubrication to prevent wet sumping, and (from 1966) Lucas electrics, better engine breathing to stem oil leaks, (1967) and coil ignition replacing the magneto ('68).

Venom Thruxton: 415%

Specials
Scrambler
In response to demand from the USA, Velocette offered Scrambler versions of the 350 and 500 in the 1950s, using the standard frame with stiffer suspension and a tuned engine. They also pioneered the two-way damped forks which later spread through the range. An Endurance version included road equipment such as a headlight. There was no specific Scrambler engine prefix, and it used the same letters as the Viper and Venom.

Sadly, the Velocette Scramblers didn't handle well off-road ("… like a camel" according to one contemporary) and didn't sell well. Consequently they are very rare and collectable today.

Scrambler: 191%

Indian Velo
The Indian Velo was an interesting aside to the Velocette story. The brainchild of Floyd Clymer, he wanted to have a bike built in Europe to suit US tastes, using the respected Indian name. Built in the Italjet factory, using mostly Italian parts (Marzzochi forks, Grimeca drum brakes), it was powered by a Venom or Thruxton engine.

The flat track styling looked odd to European eyes, but it was popular in North America at the time, and the bike was claimed to weigh 45lb less than a standard Venom. Sadly, Clymer died before the project really got off the ground, and only 250 Indian Velos were made. The final batch of 50 were bought by UK Velocette dealer Geoff Dodkin in 1971 after Velocette had closed.

Indian Velo: 305%

Venom-Metisse
Velocette enthusiasts carried on racing and enjoying the bikes after the factory closed, and a few Venom-Metisses were built in the early 1970s, marrying the Venom engine with a Metisse chassis. If you can find one, the price will be high.

Indian Velo was made in Italy, aimed at the US market. (courtesy Corey Levenson, taken at the Barber Motorsports Museum)

5 Before you view

– be well informed

To avoid a wasted journey, and the disappointment of finding that the bike does not match your expectations, it will help if you're very clear about what questions you want to ask before you pick up the phone. Some of these points might appear basic, but when you're excited about the prospect of buying your dream bike, it's amazing how some of the most obvious things slip the mind. Also check the current values of the model that interests you, in the classic bike magazine classified ads and online.

Where is the bike?

Is it going to be worth travelling to the next county/state, or even to another country? A locally advertised machine, although it may not sound very interesting, can add to your knowledge for very little effort, so make a visit – it might even be in better condition than expected.

Dealer or private sale

Establish early on if the bike is being sold by its owner or by a trader. A private owner should have all the history, so don't be afraid to ask detailed questions. A dealer may have more limited knowledge of the bike's history, but should have some documentation. A dealer may offer a warranty/guarantee, make sure to ask for a printed copy.

Cost of collection and delivery

A dealer may well be used to quoting for delivery. A private owner may agree to meet you halfway, but only agree to this after you have seen the bike at the vendor's address to validate the documents. Conversely, you could meet halfway and agree the sale, but insist on meeting at the vendor's address for the handover.

View – when and where

It is always preferable to view at the vendor's home or business premises. In the case of a private sale, the bike's documentation should tally with the vendor's name and address. Arrange to view only in daylight, and avoid a wet day, as the vendor may be reluctant to let you take a test ride if it's wet.

Reason for sale

Do make it one of the first questions. Why is the bike being sold and how long has it been with the current owner? How many previous owners?

Condition

Ask for an honest appraisal of the bike's condition. Ask specifically about some of the check items described in Chapter 7.

All original specification

As mentioned elsewhere, it's quite easy to swap parts between Velocettes and upgrade, say, an MSS into a Venom or a Venom into a Clubman, and there was a wide range of factory-fitted options, which made the original spec less cut and dried than it could be. So finding a completely original Velo may be harder than you think.

Matching data/legal ownership
Do frame, engine numbers and licence plate match the official registration document? Is the owner's name and address recorded in the official registration documents?

For those countries that require an annual test of roadworthiness, does the bike have a document showing it complies (an MoT certificate in the UK, which can be verified on 0845 600 5977) Pre-1960 bikes do not require an MoT in the UK.

Also in the UK, bikes registered in 1976 or earlier are exempt from VED (Vehicle Excise Duty, better known as 'road tax') which happily applies to all Velocettes.

Does the vendor own the bike outright? Money might be owed to a finance company or bank: the bike could even be stolen. Several organisations will supply the data on ownership, based on the bike's licence plate number, for a fee. Such companies can often also tell you whether the bike has been 'written-off' by an insurance company. In the UK these organisations can supply vehicle data:
HPI – 01722 422 422 – www.hpicheck.com
AA – 0870 600 0836 – www.theaa.com
RAC – 0870 533 3660 – www.rac.co.uk
Other countries will have similar organisations.

Unleaded fuel
With leaded fuel unavailable for many years now, many bikes will have been converted to use unleaded, or owners will use an additive. High compression engines may need an octane booster as well.

Insurance
Check with your existing insurer before setting out, as your current policy might not cover you if you do buy the bike and decide to ride it home.

How you can pay
Electronic transfer via internet banking is the quickest means of paying, and avoids waiting for a cheque to clear. Some sellers still prefer good old-fashioned cash, or may not want to email their bank details to you. The most secure way to transfer details is verbally over the phone, with the buyer inputting them directly onto his/her internet banking screen.

Buying at auction?
If the intention is to buy at auction see Chapter 10 for further advice.

Professional vehicle check (mechanical examination)
There are often marque/model specialists who will undertake professional examination of a bike on your behalf. Owners clubs may be able to put you in touch with such specialists

6 Inspection equipment

– these items will really help

This book
Reading glasses (if you need them for close work)
Overalls
Camera/smartphone
Compression tester
A friend, preferably a knowledgeable enthusiast

Before you rush out of the door, gather together a few items that will help as you work your way around the bike. This book is designed to be your guide at every step, so take it along and use the check boxes to help you assess each area of the bike you're interested in. Don't be afraid to let the seller see you using it.
Take your reading glasses if you need them to read documents and make close up inspections.

Be prepared to get dirty. Take along a pair of overalls, if you have them, and a camera or smartphone, so that later you can study some areas of the bike more closely. Take a picture of any part of the bike that causes you concern, and seek a friend's opinion.

Ideally, have a friend or knowledgeable enthusiast accompany you: a second opinion is always valuable.

Always look for the engine number – the 'R' of the VR prefix is just visible, making this a Viper engine.

Engine/frame numbers

Engine and frame numbers are key to ascertaining which model the bike was originally, and what year it left the factory. Unlike Triumphs, for example, the numbers do not match (except on military machines), so you can't use them to check whether you're looking at an original engine and frame that left the factory together.

The engine number is found just below the cylinder barrel, on the left-hand side, with a prefix to denote the model – MAC and MSS are self-explanatory, while VM, VR and VMT translate as a Venom, Viper and Thruxton respectively. A 'C' on the end of the number denotes coil ignition. Frame numbers are on the right-hand side of the upper front engine lug on rigid frames, and on a raised oblong above the head steady bracket on swingarm frames – prefixes are M for rigid and RS for swingarm.

Are the numbers clearly visible or do they look fuzzy and tampered with? If the frame has been repainted (especially if it's been powder coated) then the number may be difficult to decipher, but tampering should be obvious. If in doubt, walk away.

Having checked the engine and frame numbers, get down on the ground and look for the inspector's marks on the underside of the crankcases. These should match each other.

Documentation

Only buy a vehicle from an individual who can prove that they are the person named in the vehicle's registration document (V5C in the UK) and, preferably, at the address shown in the document. Also check that the VIN or chassis number/frame and engine numbers of the car/motorcycle match the numbers in the registration document.

An annual roadworthiness certificate (the 'MoT' in the UK) is handy proof not just that the bike was roadworthy when tested, but if there's a whole sheaf of them it gives evidence of the bike's history – when it was actively being used, and what the mileage was. The more of these that come with the bike, the better.

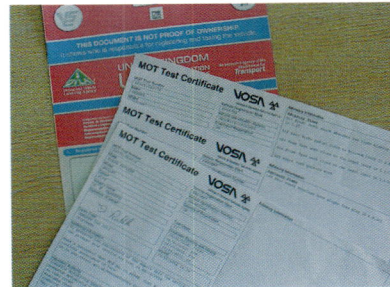

Do the engine/frame numbers match up with the documentation?

Beware upgraded bikes

We've mentioned elsewhere that it is relatively easy to upgrade one Velocette model into another simply by adding the appropriate parts. Some Vipers became Venoms after fitting the 500cc piston, barrel and cylinder head, and the addition of the correct extras turns a Venom into a Clubman.

There's nothing wrong with any of this if the seller is honest about it, stating what model the bike started out as, but that it has certain non-standard parts. After all, it's an honourable tradition among Velocette owners to fettle the bikes, and good quality parts, fitted well, won't detract from the

What's your general impression – honest patina or quickly polished up to sell?

bike's value. Problems arise when sellers try to pass off these upgraded bikes as genuine. The unscrupulous could try and dress up a standard Venom as a far more valuable Thruxton – look for that VMT engine number prefix. Bikes purporting to be Scramblers are less easy to police, since they didn't have a specific prefix – if in doubt, ask the Velocette Owners' Club if it can identify a Scrambler from the engine and frame numbers.

General condition

Put the bike on its centre stand, to shed equal light on both sides, and take a good, slow walk around it. If it's claimed to be restored, and has a nice shiny tank and engine cases, look more closely – how far does the 'restored' finish go? Are the nooks and crannies behind the gearbox as spotless as the fuel tank? If not, the bike

Ten minutes' examination shows this to be a straightforward MAC in good condition.

may have been given a quick smarten up to sell. A generally faded look all over isn't necessarily a bad thing – it suggests a machine that hasn't been restored, and isn't trying to pretend that it has.

Now look at the engine, which is by far the most expensive and time-consuming thing to put right if anything's wrong. Expect some oil leakage from the primary chain cover and/or pushrod tube, though the engine shouldn't be very oily.

Take the bike off the centre stand and stand astride it to kickstart the engine, or if you're not confident, ask the owner to do it – they should have the right knack, and if they can't start it within half a dozen kicks, then something could be wrong. Once running, the engine should rev crisply and cleanly without showing blue or black smoke. Velocettes are relatively quiet mechanically, but listen for rumbles and knocks from the bottom end. While the engine's running, check that the ammeter is showing a positive charge.

Switch off the engine and put the bike back on its centre stand. Check for play in the forks, headstock and swingarm, and the front forks or rear shocks for leaks.

Wet sumping – oil slowly draining into the crankcase while the bike is standing for long periods isn't unknown. If this has happened, the primary chaincase will have filled with oil, and then overflowed through the driveside main bearing onto the garage floor. Many owners fit a more efficient one-way valve to prevent wet sumping, or even a tap on the main oil feed (risky, if an absent-minded owner forgets to turn it on before starting up).

Are the bolt or screw heads chewed or rounded-off? Any damage to casings around bolt heads? Has someone attacked fixings with a hammer and chisel? These are signs of a careless previous owner with more enthusiasm than skill, and a dash of youthful impatience. No one has tried to butcher this bolt, though.

Listen to the engine running. Clonks or rumbles from the bottom end indicate that the main or big-end bearings are worn. Excessive blue smoke will mean a worn top end.

While the engine's running, take it up to a fast idle and check the ammeter. If there's no positive charge, the cause could be as simple as a slipping dynamo belt, or something more serious.

Something to check on the test ride. Select first gear – is the clutch dragging? Out on the road, is it slipping? Maladjustment by the owner is the usual cause, but clutches do require careful setting up.

9 Serious evaluation
– 30 minutes for years of enjoyment

Circle the Excellent (4), Good (3), Average (2) or Poor (1) box of each section as you go along. The totting up procedure is detailed at the end of the chapter. Be realistic in your marking!

All engine numbers are stamped below the cylinder barrel, left-hand side.

Frame number on a swingarm bike (hence the 'RS' prefix), on raised oblong just behind the fuel tank.

Engine/frame numbers   [1]

Engine and frame numbers are mentioned several times in this book, and for good reason. As long as they haven't been tampered with (something which is fairly obvious if it's been attempted) they will tell you which model the engine comes from. Some classic bikes, such as Triumphs and the final BSAs, are advertised as having 'matching numbers' ie that the engine and frame have the same number and were put together at the factory. Apart from machines built for the military during World War II, Velocette numbers aren't like that, but using the guide on pages 58-59 will help you confirm the model and year.

Engine numbers are on the left-hand side of the crankcase, next to the dynamo cover. On swingarm frames, the frame number is located just behind the fuel tank on the right-hand side, on a raised oblong just above the head steady bracket. On rigid frames, the number is on the right-hand side of the upper front engine lug. Take a good look at the numbers, which should match the bike's documentation. Frame numbers may be obscured if the frame has been repainted, but they should still be visible. If any numbers look fuzzy, then they may have been tampered with.

Frame number prefixes only distinguish between a rigid frame (prefix M) and swingarm (prefix RS), which will be obvious anyway. The actual number will give an indication of the year, but not a cast iron one as frames were not always used consecutively after having been numbered.

The engine number is more helpful, being specific to the model of bike: MAC and MSS prefixes are obvious, while VR denotes a Viper, VM a Venom and VMT a Thruxton. Scramblers used the same prefixes as the road bikes – VR for the 350, VM for the 500. A 'C' on the end of the number denotes one of the final engines with coil ignition. Finally, it's worth examining the underside of the crankcases for the original inspector's marks, which if they match will confirm that the two case halves were put together at the factory. If they don't, you may still have a perfectly serviceable engine, but it won't be 100% original.

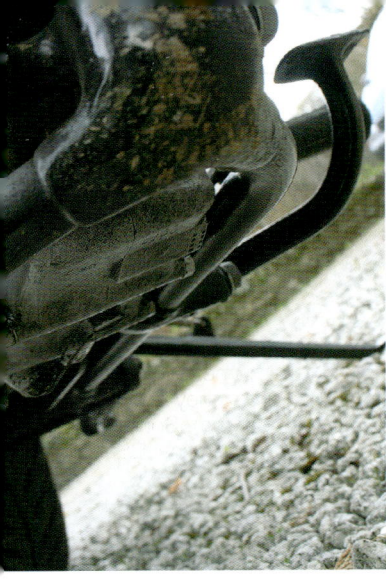

Crankcase inspection numbers (just visible here on underside of the cases) should match.

Paint

4 3 2 1

Velocettes had a good reputation for quality, and by and large it was deserved. When new, the bikes cost more than the equivalent BSA or AMC single, but that did show up in the finish as well as the mechanical parts. The original paint was good, and should have lasted well. If it has faded, that doesn't really matter if it's consistent across the bike and fits in with its general patina – better that than something with a very shiny tank and shabby side panels. Look out for quick resprays and poorly-applied coachlines.

Traditionalists love the black with gold lining which is considered the classic Velocette colour scheme, but there were others, notably the Willow Green of 1950s MACs, the pale blue Viper/Venom Specials, and the silver/blue combination used on the first Thruxtons. The actual colour doesn't seem to affect value so much as its general condition, and whether it's the original hue.

Original paint was pretty good, though many bikes have been repainted.

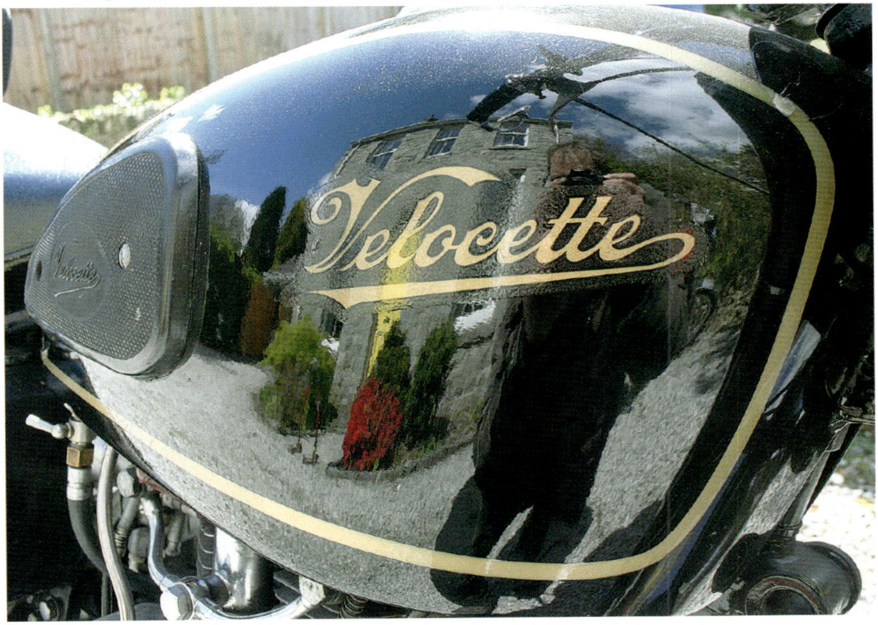

Chrome 4 3 2 1

Velocette did its own chrome plating in-house, and again the quality was pretty good from new, but age will inevitably have taken a toll. Minor blemishes can be polished away, but otherwise you're looking at a replating bill. If the silencer is seriously rotted, it's a better idea to budget for a new one – less hassle than getting the old one replated, in any case.

The various Velocette singles differed greatly in the amount of chrome applied –

Don't forget to check the condition of the knee pads.

just the handlebars and wheel rims on the MAC, MSS and the Viper/Venom Specials, but the standard Viper and Venom were far more flamboyant, with chrome mudguards and tank panels, as well as the bars and rims. The Viper/Venom Clubman and the Thruxton all had alloy rims, while other bikes stuck to chrome-plated steel

The chrome lasts pretty well.

Minor blemishes aren't worth worrying about unless you really want a concours bike.

rims. But, as ever, many owners have upgraded their bikes over the years with alloy rims and maybe stainless steel spokes. Whilst strictly speaking they're not original, they do make any bike far smarter all year round, with less effort.

Tinwork/fibreglass 4 3 2 1

In one respect, buying a secondhand bike is far easier than purchasing a used car; there's far less bodywork to worry about. Velocettes added a few parts: the usual fuel tank, mudguards and side panels, notably the clutch sprocket cover, and the headlight nacelle on the MSS, Viper and Venom.

Mudguard stays, both front and rear, can fracture through a combination of vibration and the mountings being too close together

Voluminous front mudguard on an MSS – firm, no fractured brackets, and rust-free.

New mudguards are available, though this bike clearly doesn't need them!

Velocettes are from the pre-plastic era, with lots of tinwork.

on the front. The fuel tank needs to be checked for leaks around the tap and along the seams, as well as dents and rust. Watch out for patches of filler. Repairing leaks means flushing it out, (which has to be thorough – you don't want any petrol vapour hanging about when the welding torch is fired up) but the fuel tank is at least easy to remove. Pinhole leaks can often be cured by Petseal, but anything more serious needs a proper repair. If the tank is beyond saving, new ones are available – oil tanks as well – though they're not cheap. On the other hand, the price of replacing an unsaveable tank could make it a good bargaining point.

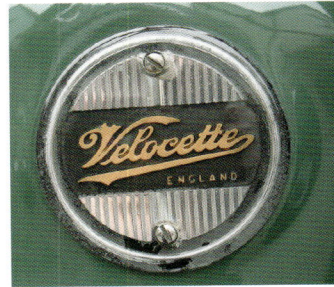

Round tank badges were fitted in the 1950s and early '60s.

Aside from the tinwork, there's also the Avon fairing on Viper and Venom Veelines. The good news is that new replicas are now available from Sprint Manufacturing, so however tatty or damaged the fairing is, you should be able to replace it. Nobody appears to be offering replacement engine enclosures, most of which were thrown away by young owners, who wanted their bike naked and unashamed. Even if the bike you are looking at is missing its enclosure, the give-away is a tag on the battery strap, other mounting points for the Dzus fasteners and dull, unpolished cases. Cracked panelling might be repairable, so it's worth keeping even if damaged.

Seat

A variety of seats were fitted to the Velocette singles – a solo sprung seat, sometimes with a separate pillion pad, on the rigid bikes, and various forms of dual seat on the swingarm machines. The dual seats had a marked step on early swingarm MACs and MSS, but most other seats were flat, plain and black – the fashion for ribbed seating seems to have passed Velocette by. The Thruxton was the only bike to sport a racing hump.

Whichever seat the bike has, the points to look for are the same. The metal pan can rust, which will eventually give way, though this is easy to check. Covers can split, which of course allows rain in, which the foam padding soaks up, and never dries out. That's a recipe for a permanently wet backside, or a rock hard seat on frosty mornings (the author speaks from experience). New covers, and complete seats in various styles are available, though recovering an old seat is a specialist job.

Original and rare, the blue humped dual seat on a silver Thruxton.

Plain black seat suited the more workaday MSS.

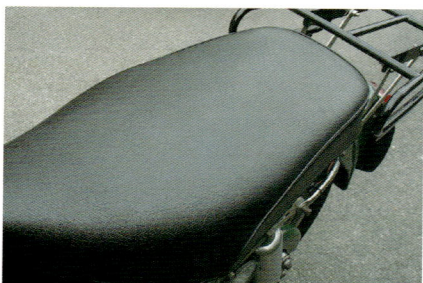

Split seat covers will let in water – this one's perfect, though.

Footrest/kickstart rubbers

Worn footrest rubbers are a good sign of high mileage, although as they're so cheap and easy to replace, not an infallible one. They should be secure on the footrest and

Nice original kickstart rubber – note the allen screw and washer added to keep it in place.

Footrest, gearchange and kickstart rubbers may have been replaced.

free of splits or tears. If the footrest itself is bent upwards, that's a sure sign the bike has been down the road at some point, so look for other telltale signs on that side. The kickstart and gearchange rubbers are also easy to replace, so well-worn ones could indicate owner neglect.

Beware the worn smooth kickstart rubber, as your foot's liable to slip off while kicking over the bike (with painful results if the lever slams back into your leg). The rubber should also be firm on the lever, and not drop off after half a dozen kicks.

Frame

All Velocette singles used variations on the same simple tubular frame, which had a single front downtube and double cradle to support the engine and gearbox. The swingarm frame was a development of the rigid item. As mentioned, it's a fine handling frame when in good condition because it is relatively lightweight and flexible.

Velocette frame is a simple tubular type, with brazed lugs in the traditional fashion.

Check as much of the frame as you can see, but the real test is in riding the bike.

However, the light weight does make them susceptible to vibration-induced fractures. The rigid MAC can crack beneath the steering head where it joins the downtube, and also where the downtube joins the cradle. The top gearbox lug on the Viper and Venom can also crack. Post-1963 bikes have a brace below the gearbox, though this, too, can break with hard track use or a crash.

As well as cracks, it's important to check whether the frame is straight and true. Crash damage may have bent it, putting the wheels out of line. One way of checking is with an experienced eye, string and a straight edge. The surest way to ascertain a frame's straightness is on the test ride – any serious misalignment should be obvious in the way the bike handles. If the wheels are out of line, it will try and drift to one side, rather than run in a straight line.

A frame that is really shabby necessitates a strip down and repaint, though as with the other paintwork, if it's original and fits in with the patina of the bike, then there's a good case for leaving it as it is.

Look for bent brackets, which can be heated and bent back into shape, and cracks around them, which can be welded.

Stands

Most bikes had both centre and sidestands (Viper/Venom Clubman and the Thruxton had a sidestand only), both of which should be secure; a loose sidestand suggests a bike that's been well used. When on the centre stand, the bike shouldn't wobble or lean: a sign of serious stand wear, and/or imminent collapse. If previous owners have been in the habit of running the bike on its stand, this won't have helped.

Well-worn side stands suggest a well-worn bike.

Most bikes (Clubman and Thruxton apart) had a centre stand as well.

Lights

Velocettes were never known for their brilliant lights, but you can at least check that the headlight, pilot light and rear/stop light are all working. Also look for a tarnished or rusted headlight reflector, which is an MoT failure, though reflectors, bulbs, glass and headlight shells are all available.

Various styles of rear light were fitted, but remember that as on all older classic bikes, only the rear brake causes the stop light to come on. One handy modification that doesn't alter the outward appearance in any way is an LED rear/stoplight bulb. This is a straight

The lights should work, but don't expect modern brilliance.

swap for the standard bulb, but won't blow, leaving you without a taillight on a dark night.

Electrics/wiring

The weakness of Velocette electrics has assumed legendary status over the years, second only to stories about the clutch. And it's true that, even by contemporary standards in the 1950s (certainly in the '60s), they were a weak link. Velocette stuck with six volts, a magneto and dynamo long after other British manufacturers had moved on, while Honda was even further ahead.

An LED stop/taillight bulb is worth fitting.

The system consists of a belt driven dynamo at the front of the cylinder barrel and a magneto behind, with voltage regulator and small battery. The magneto, which provides the sparks, has the advantage of working with a flat battery, although the strength of the spark is often weak at starting speeds. The Miller dynamo has a very low 36-watt output (though 50 watts was optional), while the voltage regulator (mounted on top of the dynamo or later the rear mudguard) can give trouble. The Miller magneto was changed to a Lucas in 1953, which is said to be better. Early dynamos used a flat-belt drive (which could slip); the later V-belt used from 1956 is more grippy.

Don't forget details like the brake light switch.

From 1968 Velocette finally switched from a magneto to coil ignition (still six volts), though this too isn't without its problems: a rotor replaced the magneto, and bearing wear in its shaft allows play, which upsets the ignition timing. A better replacement is now available.

Is the system charging? An ammeter on all bikes is a very useful instrument.

The system can be made reliable, and the good news is that there are plenty of means of improving it, with many owners doing just that. An electronic magneto, a straight replacement for the standard unit, will give a full strength spark for starting, and an electronic voltage regulator will improve reliability. For regular road use (especially if venturing out after dark), the preferred option is a full 12-volt conversion, preferably using an alternator of 120 or 180 watts. As the alternator is belt driven, car units can be fitted, and some owners have fitted the Citroën 2CV alternator. A toothed-belt drive conversion is available, but some think this doesn't offer any great advantage.

Whatever system the bike has, how readily the bike starts is a good indication of how well the electrics are working. Check that the ammeter is showing a positive charge at moderate revs, and that the dynamo belt is

Is the wiring neat and well routed?

Modern electronic magneto is a good investment for long-term ownership.

clean, properly tensioned and not perished. Batteries can suffer from vibration, as the battery box bolts directly to the engine mounting plates. Even if sensible modifications have been done, the electrical system still needs checking. A good general indication of the owner's attitude is the condition of the wiring; is it tidy and neat, or flopping around?

Wheels/tyres

On bikes with steel rims, check the chrome (rechroming entails a complete dismantle and rebuild of the wheel) and ensure that the rim is straight on all wheels. It's easy to spin the wheel and check for straightness while the bike is on its centre stand. Check none of the spokes are loose, and give each one a gentle tap with a screwdriver – any that are 'off-key' need retensioning.

Tyres should have at least the legal minimum of tread. In the UK that's at least 1mm depth, across at least three-quarters of the breadth of the tyre. Beware of bikes that have been left standing (especially on the sidestand) for some time, allowing the tyres to crack and deteriorate – it's no reason to reject the bike, but a good lever to reduce the price. New tyres in suitable sizes are no problem at all, and modern grippy tyres will fit.

Wheel sizes will take modern tyres.

Check the chrome on steel-rimmed wheels.

There shouldn't be any loose spokes.

Rear wheel bearing check.

Wheel bearings

4 3 2 1

Wheel bearings aren't expensive, but
fitting them is a hassle, and if there's
play it could affect the handling. To
check front wheel bearings, put the bike
on its centre stand, put the steering on
full lock and try rocking the front wheel
in a vertical plane, then spin the wheel
and listen for signs of roughness. Do
the same for the rear wheel. If they
do need replacing, try to find sealed
replacements, which will last longer.

Steering head 4 3 2 1
bearings

Again, the bearings don't cost an arm
or a leg, but trouble here can affect the
handling, and changing them is a big
job. With the bike on the centre stand,
swing the handlebars from lock to lock.
They should move freely, with not a
hint of roughness or stiff patches – if
there is, budget for replacing them. To
check for play, apply the front brake

**Steering head bearings are in here; note
grease nipple on this bike.**

Swingarm bearing check.

hard and attempt to rock the bike gently back and forth. Taper roller bearings are a worthwhile conversion, and if the owner has done this, that's a good sign.

Swingarm bearings

Another essential for good handling is the swingarm bearings. To check for wear, take hold of the rear wheel and try rocking the complete swing arm from side to side, feeling for any movement at the pivot. There should be nothing perceptible, but, if there is, haggle on the price, as replacement is a difficult job. The standard bearings are phosphor bronze bushes, which need to be kept greased – to eliminate greasing, nylon bushes on a stainless steel pin are the modern substitute.

Suspension

Velocette suspension is conventional for a postwar British motorcycle, the exceptions being the Dowty air forks and the slotted mount adjustment for the rear shocks. Fitted from 1948, the air forks used air pressure instead of a spring, topped up via a valve with a bicycle pump. If the seals are leaky, they lose air pressure and begin to droop – new seals are available, and some owners have fitted Triumph fork springs to avoid the problem.

Velocette's own telescopic forks were fitted from 1951. These were shrouded, and only the Thruxton and Viper/Venom Clubman MkII had gaitered forks. Pump the forks up and down to check that they work smoothly and without clonks; in good condition, they work well. Check for play by grabbing the bottom of the forks, and try to rock them backwards and forwards. Any movement indicates worn bushes, though it's easy to confuse this with movement at the steering head – there shouldn't be any play in either, of course.

Examine the forks for fluid leaks, and in particular check the soldered bottom

Shrouded forks as fitted to MAC, MSS, Viper and Venom.

Fully shrouded shock and arcuate slot for adjustment were unique to Velocette.

Webb girder forks on 1946 MSS: make sure to check that none of the bearings are loose (spares are available).

Try moving the forks back and forth, which can highlight wear in the steering head bearings as well as the fork bushes.

fork lug. This can crack under the stress of braking torque, and oil leaking from here is a warning sign. The only cure is a complete fork strip and resolder, which can be done by a specialist. On bikes with clip-ons, check that the top yokes haven't been damaged by a ham-fisted fitting. On older machines with girder forks, check the various joints for play: these should have been kept well greased.

Check the fork lower lug for cracks and leaks.

One of Velocette's most distinctive features on swingarm bikes is the arcuate slot mounting for the top of the rear shocks. The original Woodhead-Monroe shocks were not adjustable for pre-load, but moving them along these slots enabled adjustment for lighter or heavier loads. It's a simple system that works well: moving the shocks forward makes them softer, and backward stiffens them.

As long as the shocks are still oil-tight, they are serviceable. Girlings were fitted from 1963, and are available as new replacements.

Instruments

Instrumentation is limited to a speedometer and ammeter on nearly all bikes. The Thruxton was the only one to have a rev counter as standard, as this was optional on the Viper/Venom Clubman. Checking the speedo works obviously has to wait for the test ride – if neither speedo nor mileometer is working, the cable is the most

All bikes have a speedometer and ammeter.

If the speedo isn't working, the cable is most likely the issue.

likely culprit, but if one of them doesn't work, then there's something wrong internally. Instrument repair is often best left to a specialist. They do wear out eventually (the speedos, not the specialists) but new ones are available.

Thruxton had a rev counter, but this was optional on the Clubman.

A battered and bent chrome bezel suggests that a previous owner has had a go themselves.

Engine/gearbox – general impression

You can learn a lot about the engine before starting it.

The condition of the engine and gearbox is the most crucial thing to ascertain. It's not that they're more prone to trouble, simply that they are the most expensive thing to put right if there are major problems. So with the bike on its centre stand, take a good look at the engine, as it is possible to learn quite a lot before you even start it.

You're mainly looking for oil leaks, stripped threads and damaged nuts and bolts. The latter are signs of careless or ham-fisted owners; although most Velos are now owned by true enthusiasts. Some of the smaller threads can strip quite easily, so keep an eye out for obviously loose fasteners.

The Amal carburettor can leak, especially the pre-Monobloc type with a separate float chamber, though some owners have upgraded to the later Concentric carb, and think this gives easier adjustment.

Oil leaks are fairly common, partly because the narrow crankcase produces a lot of internal compression, which forces oil out through the joints. The primary chaincase is a particular culprit, as crankcase compression breathes into the case. The case is difficult to seal, though if the engine is taken apart, refacing all the joints will aid oil tightness, as will upgrading to the later breathing system used from 1967 – if the owner

Make sure to look for oil leaks and signs of neglect.

Are there any fuel leaks around the carb? This one is perfect.

has already done this, that's a good omen. If the primary drive appears to be full of oil, the engine may be wet sumping, oil draining through from the tank while the bike is standing unused. This can fill the primary case, and then overflow as a leak. Primary case leaks can also be caused by overfilling the gearbox.

The pushrod tube is also prone to leak, partly down to its two-piece telescopic design, though a one-piece tube conversion (sealed by O-rings) is available from the specialists. The kickstart shaft can leak, as there's no seal, though the outer cover can be machined to accept one.

Finally, check around the oil tank for leaks – these can be more serious, indicating that the tank has fractured where it mounts directly onto the gearbox plates, and is vulnerable to vibration.

Engine details like this (a very neat breather exit) are the sign of a skilled and fastidious owner.

While looking underneath the bike, check that the suction filter plug is intact, this sticks out proud of the crankcase and is vulnerable to damage when wheeling the bike up a kerb; especially on rigid bikes which have less ground clearance.

Ask the owner what sort of oil they use – Velocettes work best with a good quality monograde lube such as Silkolene, 30 grade in winter, 40 in summer.

Many of the same comments apply to the gearbox, look out for chewed fasteners and signs of neglect. Remove the oil filler cap and stick a finger inside to check whether the oil has been changed recently, is it nice clean lube … or a frothy sludge?

Engine – starting/idling

As mentioned on page 6, the Velocette starting ritual has acquired mythical status which puts off some people trying one. Big four-stroke singles can be awkward to start, and these bikes can be further handicapped by a weak magneto, slipping clutch and the low-geared kickstart.

But most owners agree that it's more about technique than sheer strength. Don't worry too much about the technique when viewing the bike, as the owner will

Decompressor is on the left-hand bar.

know (or should do) what works best for that particular machine. It's worth pointing out that although the lower compression MAC and MSS are easier to start than the more powerful singles, there are also variations from bike to bike. For example, you might find a Thruxton that's easier to start than a standard Venom.

Velocettes are not inherently reluctant starters, and if the fuelling and ignition are set up right, and the owner is

Ask the owner to start the bike first as they should have developed the right technique.

confident with the right technique, then they should fire up within two or three kicks, certainly when warm. If starting is difficult, then the magneto could be at fault (these can be rewound, at a price) or the culprit could be worn valve guides or general top end wear.

Once it's running, the engine should settle down to a nice steady idle, except on Thruxtons (and anything else) with a GP carburettor, which isn't expected to provide a reliable idle. Uneven running and idling can also be caused by poor adjustment of the carb, whichever type it is, or air leaks between carb and inlet tract.

Engine – smoke/noise

As mentioned, Velocette singles are strong engines, especially in the bottom end, capable of very high mileages if looked after and given regular oil changes. But they're not immune from mechanical problems. The timing side roller main bearing, which needs a precise amount of pre-load when fitted, has been known to fail spectacularly, (albeit under racing conditions) and the MAC one-piece crankpin can fail.

Old air-cooled engines can seem mechanically noisy and clattery compared to a modern liquid-cooled unit, even when running properly.

Not a Velocette, but blue smoke looks the same, whatever the bike.

But the Velocettes are mechanically fairly quiet anyway, thanks to good build quality, the belt-driven dynamo and helix-cut timing gears, which are replaced as a set and lapped in. So if you can hear the timing gears whirring noisily, it's likely that individual gears have been replaced without lapping in.

Listen for bottom end knocks – these are more noticeable on acceleration than when blipping the throttle, so it's best to wait for the test ride. Knocks or grinding could just be a slack crankshaft shock absorber, rather than terminal wear and the need for a crankshaft overhaul. But of course you won't know which it is, and it's not worth buying a bike making such suspicious noises unless it's offered at a very good price. A chuffing sound suggests the valves need reseating. If it does come to a rebuild, all engine parts are available.

Belt-drive for dynamo (under this cover).

Now look back at the silencer and blip the throttle. Blue smoke means the engine is burning oil and is a sign of general wear in the top end, with pistons/rings and valves/guides the culprits. That usually means a rebuild and, again, parts (including oversize pistons) are available. Black smoke, indicating rich running, is less of a problem, caused by carburettor wear.

Primary drive

While the engine is running, listen for clonks or rumbles from the primary drive. There are no fundamental weaknesses here so we're looking out for general wear. Primary chain adjustment may have been neglected, so rattling could be nothing more scary than a loose chain. Check the tension via the inspection hole, and there should be about 15mm of free play in the chain, between the sprockets. If the engine sprocket splines are worn, then that can

Primary chaincase won't necessarily leak – but some do.

result in chattering. Of course, you won't know the cause of undiagnosed noises without taking the primary drive cover off, but if the seller acknowledges that a noise is there, it's another good lever to reduce the price.

Chain/sprockets

With the engine switched off, examine the final drive chain and sprockets. Is the chain clean, well lubed and properly adjusted? The best way to check how worn it is is to take hold of a link and try to pull it backwards away from the sprocket. It should only reveal a small portion of the sprocket teeth – any more, and it needs replacing.

Check sprocket teeth as well as the chain.

Check chain by pulling it backwards away from the sprocket.

Check the rear sprocket teeth for wear, if they have a hooked appearance, then the sprocket needs replacing. Ditto if any teeth are damaged or missing. If the rear sprocket needs replacing, then the gearbox sprocket will too. One advantage of the Velocette inboard clutch: at least it means that the gearbox sprocket is easier to get to.

Battery

Now check the battery, it is easily accessible on the left-hand side, hidden behind a cover on later bikes. It should be securely in place, with no leaks, and with the electrolyte topped up.

Engine/gearbox mountings

These need to be completely solid, with no cracks, and no missing or loose bolts – if not, the bike is not in a rideable condition.

Modern batteries can hide inside period cases.

Exhaust

The famous fishtail silencer, which almost all Velocette singles were fitted with (the exception was the 1953 swingarm MAC), is central to the bike's appearance. UK exhaust specialist Armours has new replacements, as well as suitable downpipes. Check that the downpipe is secure in the cylinder head, as looseness causes air leaks. Examine all joints for looseness and leaks, all of which are MoT failures. The silencer should be secure, firmly mounted and in solid condition.

Test ride

The test ride should not be less than 10 minutes, and you should be doing the riding. It's understandable that some sellers are reluctant to let a complete stranger loose on their pride and joy, but

All mountings must be crack-free and bolted tight.

Expect some bluing on the downpipe, especially on harder-ridden bikes.

Fishtail silencer is a Velocette trademark, and new ones are available.

it does go with the territory of selling a bike, and, so long as you leave an article of faith (usually the vehicle you arrived in), then all should be happy. Make sure to take your driving licence in case the seller wants to see it.

Engine – performance

If you haven't ridden an older British bike before, a Velocette can take some getting used to. The MAC will feel ponderous compared to a modern 250. But, although power figures are low by modern standards (44bhp for the Thruxton and just 15bhp for the rigid MAC), these bikes do have torque, and they should still pull cleanly and without hesitation from low revs. The Viper, Venom and Thruxton in particular should rev quite freely, with good acceleration through the gears up to 60-70mph. Their extra performance will only really come in when the engine is spinning, say over 4000rpm. Whichever model it is, listen for any knocks from the bottom end when accelerating hard from low/medium revs.

Big four-stroke singles have a reputation for vibration, but the Velos are smoother than most, especially the 350s. If built up carefully they should all be reasonably smooth up to 50-55mph in top gear, but inevitably there will be vibration as speed and revs build; this is normal.

Even the basic MAC should give reasonable on-road performance.

Clutch

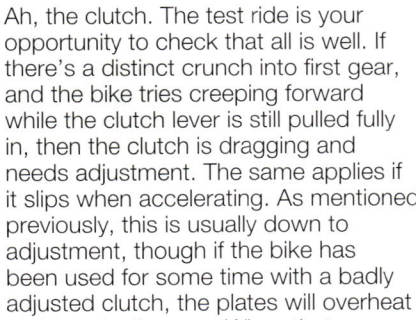

Ah, the clutch. The test ride is your opportunity to check that all is well. If there's a distinct crunch into first gear, and the bike tries creeping forward while the clutch lever is still pulled fully in, then the clutch is dragging and needs adjustment. The same applies if it slips when accelerating. As mentioned previously, this is usually down to adjustment, though if the bike has been used for some time with a badly adjusted clutch, the plates will overheat and eventually warp. When that happens, the only answer is a new set.

Even if the clutch is set up perfectly, don't expect to easily find neutral at a standstill, and in any case it's always best to follow advice and slip out of gear before the bike rolls to a stop, which gives the clutch an easier time.

Clutch in and select first gear; is there any sign of clutch drag?

Gearbox

Velocette pioneered positive stop gearchanges, and these singles have a change mechanism barely changed from the 1920s. The military bikes were one up, three down for standardisation, but all civilian machines are the more usual one down, three up. The box has a long travel but nice change, and is generally reliable, though high mileage bikes can sometimes jump out of gear, especially from first. On the test ride, go right through the gears and accelerate, then decelerate in each one to check this doesn't happen.

It's also worth checking the underside of the gearbox for cracks, especially on rigid bikes with their less generous ground clearance. Also check the gearbox locating and adjustment bolts – if these have been allowed to loosen off, then chain slack can cause damage to the castings.

Handling

Velocettes have a good reputation for handling, and it's well deserved. These are relatively light bikes with stiff suspension. They are reasonably agile and fun on twisty roads, and this applies just as much to the MAC as the Venom or Thruxton. Rigid bikes will be more upset by mid-corner bumps, but they do recover well. All of them have light, precise steering and are very responsive.

So any vagueness or weaving is not inherent and is usually down to worn forks, rear shocks or tyres. Velocette singles should never feel soft and wallowy. If they do, the suspension condition is your first thing to re-check. If the bike pulls to one side in a straight line, the wheels may be out of line or the frame could be bent. If in doubt, don't buy.

Brakes

If Velocette handling has a good reputation, then the opposite is true of the early brakes, especially the part-width front drum on the MAC and MSS. The full-width hub brakes fitted to the Viper and Venom (and optional on the MSS) were much better. But for modern traffic the Thruxton's twin-leading shoe is really the one to have, and will fit the standard full-width hub.

Having said that, the rear drum is acceptable, and even the early front drum is up to MoT standard. It just needs to be borne in mind when riding, using anticipation and not relying on the brakes to get out of trouble. That apart, the brakes aren't especially trouble-prone. They can crack in the cast iron section, and if the lever or pedal oscillates with the brake on lightly, then the drum is ovalled and will need skimming to make it round again.

Thruxton's twin leading-shoe drum is the ultimate Velocette factory brake.

Cables

All the control cables: brakes, clutch, throttle, decompressor and (if fitted) ignition advance/retard, should work smoothly, without stiffness or jerking. Poorly lubricated, badly adjusted cables are an indication of general neglect; the same goes for badly routed cables.

Switchgear

Switchgear is simple in the extreme, with just a light on/off switch (either on the

Full-width hub brakes were better than the early part-widths.

nacelle or in the headlight shell) horn and dip switches. If you haven't already, check that they work. Non-working switches could be down to something as simple as a loose connection or dirty

Early part-width drums are marginal for modern heavy traffic.

internal connections. Either way, it's something to bargain with, but, if required, new switches are available.

There are several control cables on a Velo: make sure you check they all work smoothly.

Switchgear is simple, but can still go wrong.

Miller headlight switch.

Evaluation procedure
Add up the points scored

150 to 160 points = excellent to almost concours class.
140 to 149 points = good to very good, shouldn't need any work doing.
120 to 139 points = average to good, rideable, usable bike, but not concours.
110 to 119 points = below average to average, and careful consideration required.
100 to 109 points = borderline money pit.
80 to 99 points = beware – it's going to cost a lot of money to put right.
79 points or less = run away, unless it's offered at a very good price.

10 Auctions
– sold! Another way to buy your dream

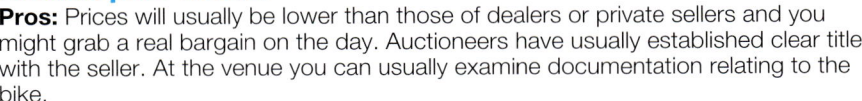

Auction pros & cons

Pros: Prices will usually be lower than those of dealers or private sellers and you might grab a real bargain on the day. Auctioneers have usually established clear title with the seller. At the venue you can usually examine documentation relating to the bike.

Cons: You have to rely on a sketchy catalogue description of condition & history. The opportunity to inspect is limited and you cannot ride the bike. Auction machines can be a little below par and may require some work. It's easy to overbid. There will usually be a buyer's premium to pay in addition to the auction hammer price.

Which auction?

Auctions by established auctioneers are advertised in the motorcycle magazines and on the auction houses' websites. A catalogue, or a simple printed list of the lots for auctions might only be available a day or two ahead, though often lots are listed and pictured on auctioneers' websites much earlier. Contact the auction company to ask if previous auction selling prices are available as this is useful information (details of past sales are often available on websites).

Catalogue, entry fee and payment details

When you purchase the catalogue of the bikes in the auction, it often acts as a ticket allowing two people to attend the viewing days and the auction. Catalogue details tend to be comparatively brief, but will include information such as 'one owner from new, low mileage, full service history,' etc. It will also usually show a guide price to give you some idea of what to expect to pay and will tell you what is charged as a 'Buyer's premium,' The catalogue will also contain details of acceptable forms of payment. At the fall of the hammer an immediate deposit is usually required, the balance payable within 24 hours. If the plan is to pay by cash there may be a cash limit. Some auctions will accept payment by debit card. Sometimes credit or charge cards are acceptable, but will often incur an extra charge. A bank draft or bank transfer will have to be arranged in advance with your own bank as well as with the auction house. No bike will be released before all payments are cleared. If delays occur in payment transfers then storage costs can accrue.

Buyer's premium

A buyer's premium will be added to the hammer price: don't forget this in your calculations. It's not usual for there to be a further state tax or local tax on the purchase price and/or on the buyer's premium.

Viewing

In some instances it's possible to view on the day or days before, as well as in the hours prior to, the auction. There are auction officials available who are willing to help out if need be. While the officials may start the engine for you, a test ride is out of the question. Crawling under and around the bike as much as you want is permitted. You can also ask to see any documentation available.

Bidding

Before you take part in the auction, decide your maximum bid – and stick to it! It may take a while for the auctioneer to reach the lot you are interested in, so use that time to observe how other bidders behave. When it's the turn of your bike, attract the auctioneer's attention and make an early bid. The auctioneer will then look to you for a reaction every time another bid is made. Usually the bids will be in fixed increments until the bidding slows, when smaller increments will often be accepted before the hammer falls. If you want to withdraw from the bidding, make sure the auctioneer understands your intentions – a vigorous shake of the head when he or she looks to you for the next bid should do the trick!

Assuming that you are the successful bidder, the auctioneer will note your card or paddle number, and from that moment on you will be responsible for the bike.

If it is unsold, either because it failed to reach the reserve or because there was little interest, it may be possible to negotiate with the owner, via the auctioneers, after the sale is over.

Successful bid

There are two more items to think about – how to get the bike home, and insurance. If you can't ride it, your own or a hired trailer is one way, another is to have it shipped using the facilities of a local company. The auction house will also have details of companies specialising in the transport of bikes.

Insurance for immediate cover can usually be purchased on site, but it may be more cost-effective to make arrangements with your own insurance company in advance, and then call to confirm the full details.

eBay & other online auctions?

eBay & other online auctions once had a reputation for bargains, though many traders as well as private sellers now use eBay and prices have risen. Velocettes, being collectable classics rising in value, tend to be sold through specialist auction houses such as Bonhams, rather than online. As with any auction, the final price depends how many buyers are bidding and how desperately they want the bike! Either way, it would be foolhardy to bid without examining the bike first, which is something most vendors encourage. A useful feature of eBay is that the geographical location of the bike is shown, so you can narrow your choices to those within a realistic radius of home. Be prepared to be outbid in the last few moments of the auction. Remember, your bid is binding and that it will be very, very difficult to get restitution in the case of a crooked vendor fleecing you – caveat emptor! Look at the seller's rating as well as the bike.

Be aware that some bikes offered for sale in online auctions are 'ghost' machines. Don't part with any cash without being sure that the vehicle does actually exist and is as described (usually pre-bidding inspection is possible).

Auctioneers

Bonhams www.bonhams.com
British Car Auctions (BCA)
www.bca-europe.com or
www.british-car-auctions.co.uk
Cheffins www.cheffins.co.uk

eBay www.eBay.com
H&H www.classic-auctions.co.uk
Shannons www.shannons.com.au
Silver www.silverauctions.com

11 Paperwork

– correct documentation is essential!

The paper trail

Older bikes sometimes come with a large portfolio of paperwork accumulated and passed on by a succession of proud owners. This documentation represents the history of the machine, from which you can deduce how well it's been cared for, how much it's been used, which specialists have worked on it and the dates of major repairs and restorations. All of this will be priceless to you, so be wary of bikes with little paperwork to support their claimed history.

Registration documents

All countries/states have some form of registration for private vehicles, such as the American 'pink slip' system or the British 'log book.' Check that the registration document is genuine, relates to the bike in question, and all the details are correct, including frame and engine numbers (if shown). If you're buying from the previous owner, their name and address will be recorded in the document: this won't be the case if you're buying from a dealer.

In the UK the current (Euro-aligned) registration document is the V5C; printed in coloured sections of blue, green and pink. The blue section relates to the motorcycle specification, the green section has details of the registered keeper (not necessarily the legal owner) and the pink section is sent to the DVLA in the UK when the bike is sold. A small section in yellow deals with selling within the motor trade.

In the UK the DVLA will can provide information about the bike for a small fee, and much can be learned in this way.

If the bike has a foreign registration there may be expensive and time-consuming formalities to complete. Do you really want the hassle? Many Velocette singles were exported to the USA, and it is possible to bring a US bike 'home' to the UK. It could be the chance to buy a bike that has only been used on dry West Coast roads, with the added glamour of a US heritage.

If the bike's still in the USA, you'll have to buy it sight unseen, and the paperwork involved in importing and re-registering is daunting. Then there's import duty on the bike, plus shipping costs, then 20% VAT on the whole lot. As there are plenty of available Velocettes, importing a bike across the Atlantic isn't worthwhile.

Roadworthiness certificate

Most countries/states require that bikes are regularly tested to prove they are safe to use on the public highway. In the UK, the 'MoT' is carried out at approved testing stations, for a fee. In the USA the requirement varies, but most states insist on an emissions test every two years as a minimum, while the police are charged with pulling over unsafe-looking vehicles.

In the UK the test is required on an annual basis for all post-1960 vehicles over three years old. Even if it isn't a legal necessity, a conscientious owner can opt to put the bike through the test anyway, as a health check. Of particular relevance for older bikes is that the certificate issued includes the mileage reading recorded at the test date and, becomes an independent record of that machine's history. Ask whether previous certificates are available. Without an MoT the bike should be trailered to its new home, unless you insist that a valid MoT is part of the deal. This is a good idea, as you will know the bike was roadworthy on the day it was tested, and you won't need to wait for the certificate to expire before having the test done.

Road licence

The administration of every country/state charges some kind of tax for the use of its road system, the actual form of the 'road licence' and, how it is displayed, varies enormously between places. The road licence must relate to the vehicle carrying it, and must be present and valid if the bike is to be ridden, legally. The value of the license will depend on the length of time it will continue to be valid.

In the UK, if a bike is untaxed because it has not been used for a period of time, the owner has to inform the licensing authorities, otherwise the vehicle's date-related registration number will be lost and there will be a painful amount of paperwork to get it re-registered. In the UK, bikes built before 1st January 1976 are road tax exempt, which applies to all factory-built Velocettes – a few machines have been built up from parts since the factory closed in 1971.

Certificates of authenticity

For many makes of older bike it is possible to get a certificate proving age and authenticity (eg engine and frame numbers, paint colour and trim). They are sometimes called 'Heritage Certificates.' If the bike comes with one, it's a definite bonus. If you want to obtain one, the owners' club is the best starting point.

Valuation certificate

The vendor may have a valuation certificate, or letter signed by a recognised expert stating how much they believe the bike to be worth (together with photos, these are usually needed to get 'agreed value' insurance). Treat these as confirmation of your own assessment, rather than a guarantee of value, as the expert may not have seen it in the flesh. Contact the owner's club to find out how to obtain a formal valuation.

Service history

Often these bikes will have been serviced at home by enthusiastic (hopefully capable) owners for a good number of years. Nevertheless, try to obtain as much service history and paperwork about the bike as you can. Specialist garage receipts score most points in the value stakes. However, anything helps in the great authenticity game, items like the original bill of sale, handbook, parts invoices and repair bills, adding to the story and the character of the machine. Even a brochure correct to the year of the bike's manufacture is useful and something you might have to search hard to find in future years. If the seller claims that the bike has been restored, then expect receipts and other evidence from a specialist restorer.

If the seller claims to have carried out servicing, ask what work was done, when, and seek evidence of it being carried out. Your assessment of the bike's condition should tell you whether the seller's claims are genuine.

Restoration photographs

If the seller tells you that the bike has been restored, then expect to be shown a series of photographs taken while the restoration was under way. Pictures taken at various stages, and from various angles, should help you gauge the thoroughness of the work. If you buy the bike, ask if you can have copies of all the photographs, as they form an important part of the history.

12 What's it worth?
– let your head rule your heart

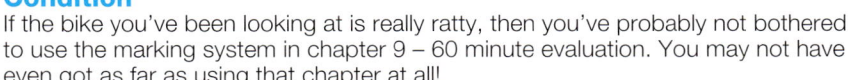

Condition

If the bike you've been looking at is really ratty, then you've probably not bothered to use the marking system in chapter 9 – 60 minute evaluation. You may not have even got as far as using that chapter at all!

If you did use the marking system in chapter 9 you'll know whether the bike is in Excellent, Good, Average or Poor condition or, perhaps, somewhere in-between these categories.

To keep-up-to date with prices, buy the latest editions of the classic bike magazines and check the classified and dealer ads, both in the magazines and online – these are particularly useful as they enable you to compare private and dealer prices. Most of the magazines run auction reports as well, which publish the actual selling prices, as do the auction house websites. Remember that the price listed for online auctions (unless it's a 'Buy it Now' price) is only the highest current bid, not the final selling price.

Velocette singles are not 'blue chip' investments, but they are still gradually increasing in value, and are very unlikely to depreciate in the near future. Even the MAC, the least glamorous Velo single and the most common in production terms, is still on the way up. The Thruxton will always command a big premium, thanks to its rarity and desirability, but other rare variants, such as the Viper/Venom Clubman MkIIs, the Scramblers and Indian Velo, will also be worth more. For each model, actual values depend more on condition than year or mileage.

Assuming that the bike you have in mind is not in show/concours condition, then relate the level of condition that you judge it to be in with the appropriate price in the adverts. How does the figure compare with the asking price?

Before you start haggling with the seller, consider what affect any variation from standard specification might have on the bike's value. This is a personal thing: for some, absolute originality is non-negotiable, while others see non-standard parts as an opportunity to pick up a bargain. Do your research in the reference books, so that you know the bike's spec when it left the factory. That way, you shouldn't end up paying a top-dollar price for a non-original bike. With Velocettes, some non-standard upgrades, such as the twin-leading shoe brake, do not seem to hurt values, and can actually increase them. If you are buying from a dealer, remember prices are generally higher than in private sales.

Striking a deal

Negotiate on the basis of your condition assessment, mileage, and fault rectification cost. Also take into account the bike's specification. Be realistic about the value, but don't be completely intractable; a small compromise on the part of the vendor or buyer will often facilitate a deal at little real cost.

13 Do you really want to restore?

– it'll take longer and cost more than you think

There's a certain romance about restoration projects, about bringing a sick bike back into blooming health, and it's tempting to buy something that 'just needs a few small jobs' to bring it up to scratch. But there are two things to think about. Firstly, once you've got the bike home and start taking it apart, those few small jobs could turn into big ones. And secondly, restoration takes time, which is a precious thing in itself. Be honest with yourself: will you get as much pleasure from working on the bike as you will from riding it?

There's nothing wrong with a good bit of honest wear.

Of course, you could hand the whole lot over to a professional, and the biggest cost involved there is not the new parts, but the sheer labour involved. Such restorations don't come cheap, and, if taking this route, there are a few other issues to bear in mind.

First, make it absolutely clear what you want doing. Do you want the bike to be 100% original at the end of the process, or simply useable? Do you want a concours finish, or are you prepared to put up with a few blemishes on the original parts?

Secondly, make sure that there is a detailed estimate involved, and that it is more or less binding. There are too many stories of a person quoted one figure only to be presented with an invoice for a far larger one!

Third, check that the company you're dealing with has a good reputation. The owners' club, or one of the reputable parts suppliers, should be able to make a few recommendations.

Finally, a ground-up restoration of a MAC or MSS could end up costing more than the finished bike will be worth. Not that this should put you off, if you have the budget, and really want to do it this way.

Restoring the bike yourself requires a number of skills, which is fine if you

Attention to detail is essential for full restorations.

50

Living with minor blemishes like this is a lot cheaper than restoring.

already have them, but if you haven't it's good not to make your newly acquired bike part of the learning curve! Can you weld? Are you confident about building up an engine? Do you have a warm, well-lit garage with a solid workbench and good selection of tools?

Be prepared for a top-notch professional to put you on a lengthy waiting list or, if tackling a restoration yourself, expect things to go wrong and set aside extra time to complete the task. Restorations can stretch into years when things like life intrude, so it's good to have some sort of target date.

There's a lot to be said for a rolling restoration,

This sort of finish, on a Viper built for hillclimbing, takes a lot of dedication to achieve ...

especially as the summers start to pass with your Velo still off the road. This is not the way to achieve a concours finish, which can only really be achieved via a thorough nut-and-bolt rebuild, without the bike getting wet and gritty in the meantime. But an 'on-the-go' restoration does have its plus points. Riding helps keep your interest up as the bike's condition improves, and it's also more affordable than trying to do everything in one go. In the long run, it will take longer, but you'll get some on-road fun out of the bike in the meantime.

14 Paint problems
– bad complexion, including dimples, pimples and bubbles

Paint faults generally occur due to lack of protection/maintenance, or to poor preparation prior to a respray or touch-up. Some of the following conditions may be present in the bike you're looking at:

Orange peel

This appears as an uneven paint surface, similar to the appearance of the skin of an orange. The fault is caused by the failure of atomised paint droplets to flow into each other when they hit the surface. It's sometimes possible to rub out the effect with proprietary paint cutting/rubbing compound or very fine grades of abrasive paper. A respray may be necessary in severe cases. Consult a paint shop for advice.

Left to itself, damaged paint will allow rust to get a toehold.

Cracking

Severe cases are likely to have been caused by too heavy an application of paint, or filler beneath the paint. Also, insufficient stirring of the paint before application can lead to the components being improperly mixed, and cracking can result. Incompatibility with the paint already on the panel can have a similar effect. To rectify it is necessary to rub down to a smooth, sound finish before respraying the problem area.

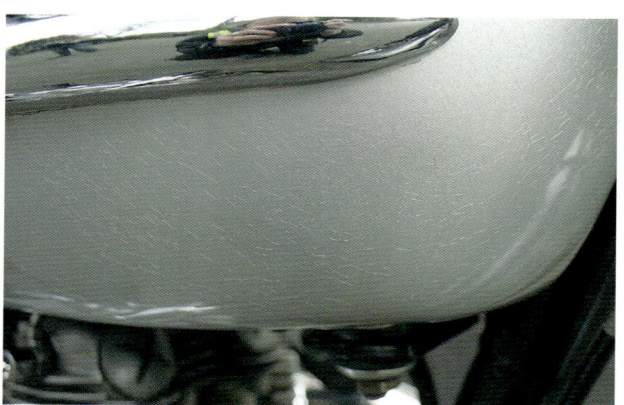

Crazed finish will need a complete repaint, if you can't live with it.

Crazing

Sometimes the paint takes on a crazed rather than a cracked appearance when the problems mentioned under 'cracking' are present. This problem can also be caused by a reaction between the underlying surface and the paint. Paint removal and respraying the problem area is usually the only solution.

Blistering

Almost always caused by corrosion of the metal beneath the paint. Usually perforation will be found in the metal and the damage will often be worse than that suggested by the area of blistering. The metal will have to be repaired before repainting.

Micro blistering

Usually the result of an economy respray where inadequate heating has allowed moisture to settle on the vehicle before spraying. Consult a paint specialist, but damaged paint will have to be removed before partial or full respraying. Can also be caused by bike covers that don't 'breathe.'

Fading

Some colours, especially reds, are pone to fading if subject to strong sunlight for long periods, without the benefit of polish protection. Sometimes proprietary paint restorers and/or paint cutting/ rubbing compounds will retrieve the situation. Often a respray is the only real solution.

Fuel stains like this should polish out.

Peeling

Often a problem with metallic paintwork when the sealing lacquer becomes damaged and begins to peel off. Poorly applied paint may also peel. The remedy is to strip and start again.

Dimples

Dimples in the paintwork are caused by the residue of polish (particularly silicone types) not being removed properly before respraying. Paint removal and repainting is the only solution.

15 Problems due to lack of use

– just like their owners, Velocettes need exercise!

Like people, Velocettes deteriorate if they sit doing nothing for long periods of time. This is especially relevant if the bike is laid up for six months of the year, as some of them are.

Rust

If the bike is put away wet, and/or stored in a cold, damp garage, the paint, metal and brightwork will suffer. Ensure the machine is completely dry and clean before going into storage, and spray with an anti-corrosion oil. If you can afford it, invest in a dehumidifier to keep the garage atmosphere dry.

Cables

Cables are vulnerable to seizure – the

Give all the controls a workout once a week or so.

Keep the battery topped up to maintain its health.

answer is to thoroughly lube them beforehand, and come into the garage to give them a couple of pulls once a week or so.

Tyres

If the bike's been left on its sidestand, most of its weight is on the tyres, which will develop flat spots and cracks over time. Always leave the bike on its centre stand, if it has one, to take weight off of the tyres.

Engine

Old, acidic oil can corrode bearings. Many riders change the oil in the spring, when they're putting the bike back on the road, but really it should be changed just before the bike is laid up, so that the bearings are sitting in fresh oil. The same goes for the gearbox. While you're giving the cables their weekly exercise, turn the engine over slowly on the kickstart, ignition off. Don't start it though, because running the engine

Eventually, even nice polished alloy like this will lose its shine.

Paintwork will, inevitably, deteriorate over time.

for a short time does more harm than good, as it produces a lot of moisture internally, which the engine doesn't get hot enough to burn off. That will attack the engine internals and the silencer.

Battery/electrics

Either remove the battery and give it a top-up charge every couple of weeks, or connect it to a battery top-up device such as the Optimate, which will keep it permanently fully charged. Damp conditions will allow fuses and earth connections to corrode, storing up electrical troubles for the spring. Eventually, wiring insulation will harden and fail.

16 The Community
– key people, organisations and companies in the Velocette world

Auctioneers
Bonhams www.bonhams.com/
Cheffins www.cheffins.co.uk/
eBay www.eBay.com/
H&H www.classic-auctions.co.uk/
Silver www.silverauctions.

Velocette owners' clubs across the world
UK – www.velocetteowners.com
France – www.velocette.fr
Germany – www.velocette.de
Netherlands – www.velocetteclub.nl
Australia – www.velocetteoz.businesscatalyst.com
New Zealand – www.velocette.org.nz
Argentina – www.facebook.com/VelocetteOwnersArgentina

Specialists
We have restricted our listing to UK companies. This list does not imply recommendation and is not deemed to be comprehensive. Don't forget the Velocette Owners Club in the UK runs its own spares scheme.
- Grove Classic Motorcycles (spares) – www.groveclassicmotorcycles.co.uk
- KTT Services (special parts) – www.kttservices.co.uk
- Alton (alternator and electric start conversions) – www.alton-france.com
- Clive Repik Restorations (restorations) – www.repik.co.uk
- Criterion (Engineers) (modified parts)
  – Email: sanjmgc@waitrose.com (01793) 796219
- Gear Set (5/6-speed gear clusters) – www.velocettegearset.com
- Sprint Manufacturing (Avon fairings) – www.triumphparts.gbr.cc
- Chronometric Instrument Services (instruments and cables)
  – Email: info@chronometrics.co.uk (0115) 920 6156

Books
NB: Some of these books are out of print, but secondhand examples are available online
Velocette Motorcycles – MSS to Thruxton, Rod Burris, Veloce Publishing
Velocette: Technical Excellence Exemplified, Ivan Rhodes, Osprey
The Velocette Saga, CE 'Titch' Allen, Amulree Publishing
Always in the Picture, Bob Burgess and Jeff Clew, Haynes Publishing

17 Vital statistics

– essential data at your fingertips

Listing the vital statistics of every Velocette variant would take more room than we have here, so we've picked three representative models: 1954 MAC, 1959 Venom and 1970 Venom Thruxton

Max speed
1954 MAC: 75mph
1959 Venom: 102mph
1970 Venom Thruxton: 110mph

Engine
1954 MAC: Air-cooled OHV single – 349cc. Bore and stroke 68 x 96mm. Compression ratio 6.75:1. Power 15bhp @ 6300rpm
1959 Venom: Air-cooled OHV single – 499cc. Bore and stroke 86 x 86mm. Compression ratio 8.0:1. Power 36bhp @ 6200rpm
1970 Venom Thruxton: Air-cooled OHV single – 499cc. Bore and stroke 86 x 86mm. Compression ratio 9.0:1. Power 41bhp @ 6200rpm

Gearbox
1954 MAC: Four-speed. Ratios: 1st 14.1:1, 2nd 9.6:1, 3rd 7.3:1, 4th 5.5:1.
1959 Venom: Four-speed. Ratios: 1st 11.24:1, 2nd 7.78:1, 3rd 5.91:1, 4th 4.9:1
1970 Venom Thruxton: Four-speed. Ratios: 1st 10.1:1, 2nd 6.97:1, 3rd 5.3:1, 4th 4.4:1

Brakes
1954 MAC: Front 7in sls (single leading shoe) drum, rear 6in sls drum
1959 Venom: Front 7.5in sls drum, rear 7in sls drum
1970 Venom Thruxton: Front 7.5in tls (twin leading shoe) drum, rear 7in sls drum

Electrics
1954 MAC: 6-volt, magneto
1959 Venom: 6-volt, magneto
1970 Venom Thruxton: 6-volt, coil ignition

Weight
1954 MAC: 355lb
1959 Venom: 390lb
1970 Venom Thruxton: 390lb

Timeline

1933 – MOV introduced
1934 – MAC introduced
1935 – MSS introduced
1940/41 – Military spec MDD and MAF for British/French armies
1946 – MOV, MAC and MSS re-introduced
1948 – Dowty air forks replace girder forks, MOV and MSS dropped
1951 – Telescopic forks replace Dowtys, alloy cylinder head
1953 – MAC swingarm frame
1954 – MSS (86 x 86mm engine, swingarm) introduced
1955 – MSS Scrambler and Endurance, with gaitered two-way damped forks
and Amal Monobloc carb
1956 – Viper and Venom launched, Endurance offered in UK, Viper Scrambler
launched, headlight nacelle on all road bikes
1957 – Racing kit for Viper and Venom
1958 – Voltage regulator moved to rear mudguard, engine covers introduced
1959 – Viper/Venom Clubman introduced
1960 – MAC dropped, dynamo uprated to 60 watts, squared-off 4.25-gallon
tank for Clubman
1961 – Veeline fairings introduced
1962 – 4.25-gallon tank on Viper/Venom
1963 – Viper/Venom Specials introduced, Woodhead-Monroe shocks
replaced by Girlings
1964 – Thruxton cylinder head optional on Venom as part of production racing kit
1965 – Thruxton introduced
1966 – Lucas electrics replace Miller
1967 – Improved engine breathing, Viper/Venom Clubman MkII, one-piece
pushrod tube, Amal Concentric carb, tank transfers (not badges) on all bikes
1968 – Coil ignition
1969 – Viper/Venom Specials dropped, Viper Clubman dropped, Indian Velo
launched
1970 – Production ends in December
1971 – Velocette closes

Engine/frame numbers

Numbers quoted are as close as possible to the start and end of each model's
production.

Engine prefixes:

MOV – MOV
MAC – MAC
MSS – MSS
Viper – VR
Venom – VM

Thruxton – VMT
Frame prefixes:
Rigid frame – M
Swingarm frame – RS

Date	Engine no	Frame no
1933	1	1
Sept 1948	6500	6062
MAC		
Dec 1933	64	605
Jan 1953	19318	12744
Swingarm frame		

Date	Engine no	Frame no
Dec 1952	20001	1001
Jul 1954	23162	5194
Remainder of MAC production		
records missing		
MSS		
May 1935	1002	21
Jun 1948	8304	10496
Swingarm frame		
Dec 1953	10001	3389
1970	13276	
MDD		
Matching engine/frame numbers 1940/41 MDD1101 to MDD12201		
MAF		
Matching engine/frame numbers 1940/41 MAF1001 to MAF1948		

Venom/Viper date	Engine no	Frame no
Dec 1955	1001	7623
Dec 1956	1537	9165
Nov 1957	1929	10233
Dec 1958	2692	11443
Dec 1959	3750C	13798
Dec 1960	5068C	16306
Dec 1961	5485	17447
Dec 1962	5562C	17553
Dec 1963	5759	17865
Dec 1964	5996C	18218
Dec 1965	6173C	18723
Oct 1966	6278	19020
Dec 1967	6449	19550
Jan 1969	6459	19636
Nov 1969	6683C	19133
Thruxton		
Jun 1965	102	18237
Dec 1966	479	19156
Dec 1967	686	19537
Dec 1968	871	19794
Dec 1969	V1088	20051
Dec 1970	1208	20177

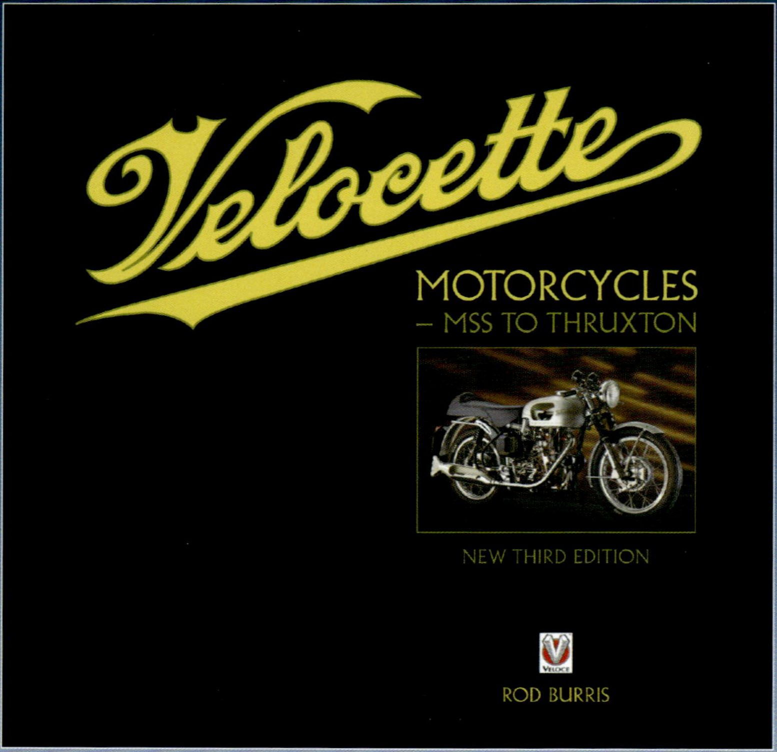

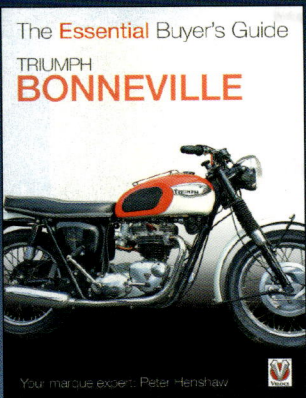
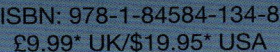

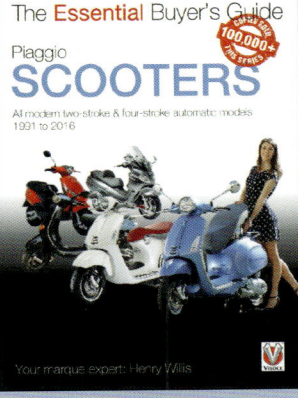

The **Essential** Buyer's Guide™ series ...

   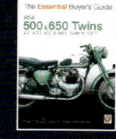   

 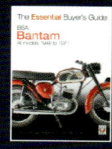 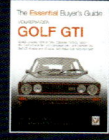    

   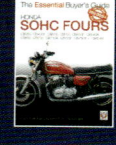 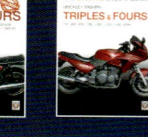 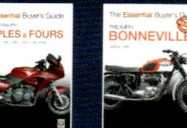 

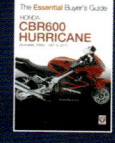    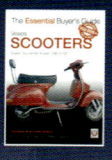  

     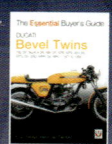